P9-DGG-651

WITHDRAWN
No longer the property of the
Boston Public Library.
Sale of this material benefits the Library

Satchel Paige

The Best Arm in Baseball

Patricia and Fredrick McKissack

Series Consultant: Dr. Russell L. Adams, Chairman,
Department of Afro-American Studies, Howard University

Illustrations by Michael David Biegel

❖ *Great African Americans Series* ❖

ENSLOW PUBLISHERS, INC.

Bloy St. & Ramsey Ave.	P.O. Box 38
Box 777	Aldershot
Hillside, N.J. 07205	Hants GU12 6BP
U.S.A.	U.K.

To Elizabeth and Gilbert Merritt

Copyright ©1992 by Enslow Publishers, Inc.

All rights reserved.

No part of this book may be reproduced by any means
without the written permission of the publisher.

Library of Congress Cataloging-in-Publication Data

McKissack, Pat, 1944-
    Satchel Paige : the best arm in baseball / Patricia and Fredrick McKissack.
      p. cm. — (Great African Americans series)
    Includes index.
    Summary: Describes the life of one of baseball's greatest pitchers, who was unable to
play major league baseball due to segregation for many years, after which he became the first
black pitcher in the American League.
    ISBN 0-89490-317-9
    1. Paige, Leroy, 1906–1982—Juvenile literature. 2. Baseball players—
United States—Biography—Juvenile literature. [1. Paige, Leroy, 1906–1982.
2. Baseball players. 3. Afro-Americans—Biography.] I. McKissack, Fredrick.
II. Title. III. Series: McKissack, Pat, 1944– Great African Americans series.
GV865.P3M36 1992
796.357'092—dc20
[B]   92-3583
                                            CIP
                                            AC

Printed in the United States of America

10 9 8 7 6 5 4 3 2 1

Photo Credits: Copyright Washington Post, Reprinted by Permission of the D.C. Public Library,
pp. 4, 14, 20, 22, 25, 28; Library of Congress, p. 7.

Illustrations Credit: Michael David Biegel

Cover Illustration: Ned O.

Contents

Leroy (Satchel) Paige
Born: July 7, 1906, Mobile, Alabama.
Died: June 8, 1982, Kansas City, Missouri.

1

Living in a Shotgun

When Satchel Paige was born he was
named Leroy Paige. Leroy grew up in a
large family. He had ten brothers and
sisters. His parents worked very, very
hard. His father earned money as a
gardener. His mother washed and ironed
clothes for money. But the family was still
poor.

The Paiges lived in a small house on
Franklin Street in Mobile, Alabama. It was
called a shotgun house. There were four

rooms, one behind the other. "A straight shot from the front door to the back," Satchel said.

When Leroy was seven years old, he earned money at the train station. He carried traveler's bags, sometimes called satchels, for money. He carried so many at one time, his friends said he was a "satchel

Downtown Mobile at the turn of the century.

tree." Pretty soon he was just called Satchel.

When he wasn't working, Satchel liked to throw things. It was fun hitting trees and cans with rocks. He became good at it. First, he took aim. Then he threw the rock. Zap! He hit the mark almost every time.

2

Mount Meigs, Alabama

Satchel didn't like school. So, he didn't go very often. Then he was caught stealing toys. In 1918, when he was twelve years old, a judge sent him to the Industrial School for Negro Children at Mount Meigs, Alabama. He stayed there until he was seventeen.

"It was the best thing that happened to me," Satchel said later. "I was running around with the wrong crowd."

At Mount Meigs, he stopped throwing

rocks and learned how to throw a baseball on the school baseball team. That was the beginning. Satchel Paige would still be throwing baseballs thirty years later.

When Satchel left Mount Meigs he was about 6 feet and 3½ inches tall. He weighed 140 pounds. "I was so tall and thin everybody called me 'The Crane,' " he said.

Satchel wanted to play baseball, so he joined the Mobile Tigers. All the players were black. Wilson Paige, one of Satchel's brothers, played for the Tigers, too. Satchel was the team's star pitcher.

3

The Traveling Man

In the 1920s the United States was segregated. There were laws that kept blacks and whites from going to school together. They could not live in the same neighborhoods. And they could not play professional sports in the same leagues. African Americans played baseball in the "Negro Leagues."

Being a Negro League ball player wasn't easy. The team traveled in old cars and run-down buses. They weren't

welcome in most hotels and restaurants.
Many times the team had to sleep on the
ball park benches.

White fans came to see the black teams
play. Sometimes those fans shouted

Satchel was a great pitcher. But, he was also a good
bunter. Here he is in a bunting position.

unkind things to the black players. But
when they saw Satchel Paige pitch, they
cheered. His best pitch was the fast ball.
He called it his "bee ball," because it
hummed like a bee. He also threw a hard
breaking curve ball and a fast slider.

In 1926, he joined the Chattanooga Black Lookouts. He earned $50 a month. "Big money for me then," Satchel said. But he was restless. He moved from team to team. From 1926 to 1934, Satchel Paige pitched for teams in Birmingham, Alabama and Cleveland, Ohio. Satchel proved how good he was with the Pittsburgh Crawfords between 1931 and 1934. Satchel helped the Crawfords win the Negro National League title in 1933.

During off-seasons, Satchel played for teams in the Caribbean, Mexico, and South America. He was known as a "traveling man."

On October 26, 1934, Satchel married Janet Howard. They did not live together very much. Satchel liked to travel. He could not settle down. Soon the marriage ended.

Now Satchel was getting older. Some people thought his pitching arm had burned out. The Kansas City Monarchs signed him to a contract anyway. The Monarchs were smart. Satchel had many more seasons left to pitch.

4

The Monarch Years

Between 1939 and 1942, the Monarchs won the Negro American League championship every year. Satchel was a big part of it. The Monarchs beat the Homestead Grays and won the Negro World Series in 1942. Satchel pitched the winning game. He was older now, but he was as good as ever.

Satchel did not make a whole lot of money. But he made more than most black ball players did in the 1940s. If Satchel

Satchel (right) with All-Star player Stan Musial (center) and Bob Feller (left). Sometimes in very special games black All-Star players would play against white All-Star players. In 1986 Bob Feller said Satchel was "as good as any pitcher today."

had been white, he would have pitched for one of the major league teams. But he could only play in the Negro Leagues.

Satchel was one of the best pitchers who ever played the game. And he was the first to say it! Satchel loved to brag as much as he liked to make people laugh. Satchel said and did funny things on and off the baseball field. One of his most famous sayings was, "Don't look back. Something might be gaining on you."

Satchel spent a lot of money, too. He went back to visit his mother in Mobile. She was still living in the same small shotgun house. One day he took her out for a ride. He showed her a large house and asked her if she liked it. She said it was

When Satchel first started playing baseball, the Negro
League teams traveled by car or bus. By the 1950s, teams
traveled in airplanes, like the one Satchel is in above.

too big. Satchel said it was hers. He had already bought it for her. At last, he moved his mother out of the shotgun shack.

Satchel's girlfriend, Lahoma Brown, wanted him to spend his money wisely. She talked him into buying a large home in Kansas City. On October 12, 1947, they were married in Hays, Kansas.

5

If He Was White

In 1947 Jackie Robinson was chosen as the first black player to start in the all-white National League. He played for the Brooklyn Dodgers.

Satchel was hurt that he had not been the first black player in the National League. He had worked long and hard for the chance to be that player. But a lot of people thought he was too old.

Satchel finally got his chance in the majors on July 9, 1948. He signed up with the Cleveland Indians. That made him the first black pitcher in the American League. At 42 years old, he was also the oldest rookie.

Satchel won six games and lost one during his first season. His team won the

Bill Veeck (right) signed a contract with Satchel (left) to have him pitch for Cleveland in 1948. In 1950 Satchel was dropped from the major league. But in 1951, Veeck brought Satchel back to his new American League team, the St. Louis Browns. Satchel pitched with the Browns for three seasons.

American League Championship. They also won the 1948 World Series against the Boston Braves.

Satchel only got to pitch one inning in the World Series. It was enough for him. He said, ". . . it felt great!" Satchel was very proud. Even at his age, he could still throw a baseball hard, fast, and straight.

Satchel retired after the 1949 season. But not for long. He played whenever he could for many more years. Finally, he became a coach for the Atlanta Braves. And in 1968, he really did retire.

All his life, Satchel had heard: "We sure could use a pitcher like you. If you were white." But he was never bitter. "I don't look back," he said often.

Satchel won many honors for his work in baseball on and off the field. His greatest honor came in August 1971.

During the 1954-55 season, Satchel did "barnstorming." That meant he played exhibition games, where he would pitch three or four games with a team and then move on to another team. In this picture Satchel was barnstorming with a Chicago team. Here he is signing copies of his autobiography *Maybe I'll Pitch Forever*.

LEROY ROBERT PAIGE
"SATCHEL"

BIEGEL

Leroy "Satchel" Paige was accepted into the Baseball Hall of Fame.

Most great Negro League baseball players were part of their own Hall of Fame. They were still segregated. Satchel Paige was a great pitcher. He was placed alongside other great major league players like Babe Ruth and Jackie Robinson. For the first time, nobody said, "If he was only white." His skin color didn't matter.

Satchel Paige lived in Kansas City with Lahoma the rest of his life. He died on June 8, 1982.

Words to Know

American League—One of two groups of major league teams that play among themselves to win a pennant. The pennant winner plays the National League pennant winner in the World Series.

Baseball Hall of Fame—A special place where baseball players are honored for their careers.

Major League—A group of professional baseball teams that play against each other for championships.

National League—One of two groups of major league teams that play among themselves to win a pennant. The pennant winner plays the American League pennant winner in the World Series.

Negro—A word that was used for African Americans at one time. It is not used much any more.

Negro Leagues—A group of all-black baseball teams who only played against each other.

Negro World Series—The top team in the Negro National League played the top team in Negro American League for the championship.

retire—To choose to stop working permanently at a regular job or profession.

satchel—An old name for a traveling bag that usually had a shoulder strap.

segregated—Separated from, apart. At one time, the United States had separate schools for blacks and whites. The races could not work together or share public accommodations, like hotels, restaurants, and restrooms.

shotgun house—A house where all the rooms are placed one behind the other. If you opened up all the doors in the house, you could shoot a shotgun through the front door and the shot would come out the other side without going through any walls.

Index